About the *Ready-to-Use Writing Workshop Activities Kits*

The *Ready-to-Use Writing Workshop Activities Kits* offer a proven and effective method for teaching the process of writing. Each of the six workshop kits contains 25 or more ready-to-use activities for improving basic writing skills in grades 4-8:

KIT I: *Word Skills* features activities with word banks and vocabulary lists that encourage students to actively use words from their listening vocabulary in writing. Parts of speech and their usage are also included, along with a clip-and-use sensory vocabulary game and a graded spelling/learning station.

KIT II: *Sentence Skills* offers exercises in using simple, compound, and complex sentences—including how to identify and generate them—as well as using figures of speech, such as similes, metaphors, and hyperbole.

KIT III: *Paragraph Writing Skills* involves the students with lessons in descriptive, persuasive, narrative, and expository writing.

KIT IV: *Editorial Skills* reinforces the students' editorial strengths. Each lesson features a specific writing improvement skill, including agreement, tenses, fragments, and run-ons.

KIT V: *Letter and Report Writing Skills* gives the students practical experience in writing both business and personal letters, preparing "workable" lists, and using some fresh approaches to report writing.

KIT VI: *Notetaking and Outlining Skills* helps students to prepare for longer writing assignments with exercises in summarizing, notetaking, and outlining.

You'll find that the *Ready-to-Use Writing Workshop Activities Kits* provide a practical four-step system for teaching that will:

- Give students frequent and varied opportunities to write
- Help students to write for a specific purpose
- Cause students to experience many styles and forms of writing, including sentences, paragraphs, lists, and summaries
- Involve students purposefully in their peers' writing
- Provide the student writer with immediate feedback from a specific audience (namely, two peers and the teacher)

Each activity is divided into two parts: "Warming Up," an introductory exercise and/or statement, and "Writing Activities," the beginning of the workshop process.

Here's how the four-step system works:

Step 1: Student prepares a rough draft using the "Writing Activities" section of an activity. Any piece of writing, at least a paragraph in length, would be suitable.

Step 2: Two peer editors are chosen by the student to read and discuss the rough draft.

Step 3: Teacher and student meet for a brief conference to assess how the writing has progressed.

Step 4: Student recopies his or her work, has the final copy checked by the teacher, and displays the completed lesson in the classroom.

You can easily and productively turn your classroom into an efficient writing workshop by reproducing several activities at one time, thereby offering your students a variety of assignments from which to choose. You may also prepare five or six activities and divide your class into groups based on need or interest. Finally, you may reproduce each activity as a single lesson for the whole class. It's a proven system that students and teachers can readily adapt according to their own needs and interests.

The *Ready-to-Use Writing Workshop Activities Kits* will challenge and delight your students. You'll find the workshop atmosphere and ready-to-use activities time-saving and conducive to learning. Your students will discover that writing *can* be a stimulating, effective, and pleasurable means of communicating!

Judith Schifferle

How to Turn Your Classroom into a Writing Workshop

Your first goal is to involve students in the four steps of the Writing Workshop System. Reproduce these pages for your students:

1. Writing Workshop Student Directions, page 6. (You may also want to make a large classroom poster of the steps for handy reference.)
2. Writing Workshop Editor's Key, page 7.
3. Editing practice activity. (A sample page and answer key can be found on pages 8 and 9. Kit IV is devoted entirely to editing. You may also reproduce your students' writing samples to provide *several* practice sessions.)

Plan large group lessons using these materials. Have the students keep the materials in individual writing folders.

You can use the *precomposing activities* from Kits I and II prior to or along with the *writing activities* from Kits III-VI. Kit I features vocabulary, parts of speech and usage, and a bonus spelling learning station. In Kit II, the skills include sentence writing and manipulation and using figures of speech.

Step 1: Rough Draft

Give your students a choice of several kinds of writing activities. If you can devote large blocks of time solely to writing, then reproduce about fifteen activities from Kits III-VI. Each activity features easy-to-follow "Warming Up" directions to help the students begin.

Once students begin producing rough drafts, they will move through the remaining three steps at their own pace. They may become involved in one or more steps during a class period. The length of a rough draft depends on the type of writing activity chosen, the grade level, and your students' abilities.

Step 2: Peer Editing

How far editors should go in making suggestions and editing is an important and sensitive issue. An editor should always point out at least one positive aspect of the writing. Develop constructive ways of criticizing and questioning. A good question from an editor will help the writer to clarify and/or expand the writing. Encourage editors to make specific comments. Decide who has the final say about suggested changes in case of disagreement.

To train editors, distribute copies of several writing samples from your class. Use the Editor's Key as the basis for class discussions on the proofreading process, or use the specially tailored exercises in Kit IV, *Editorial Skills*. Schedule weekly large group practice lessons that highlight a specific skill or reproduce lessons according to students' needs.

Have both editors sign their names to the rough draft. This will help you identify who the most effective editors are. See the practice activity on page 9 for the recommended heading.

Note: Requiring *two* editors is practical and workable because it gives the writer different responses and feedback in a minimum amount of time. Also, students are less self-conscious about working with one or two students at a time than if they were to read their writings in front of the entire class.

Students with weak reading and language skills may begin by dictating their writing to another student or onto a tape, which can be transcribed later. All writers should read their stories *aloud* to at least one of their editors and accept written and verbal comments and questions.

Be aware of your students' attitudes toward reading and editing another student's work. Use the reproducible survey on page 10 to help keep the lines of communication open. Plan a group discussion to discuss the results of the survey once the Writing Workshop System has been in use for a few weeks.

Step 3: Student/Teacher Conferences

Meet individually for three to five minutes with your students after they have completed Steps 1 and 2. Just as the two student editors have done, focus on at least one specific positive feature of the student's writing, such as an effective opening. Then pick one aspect that could be strengthened. Kits III and V contain reproducible checklists that will help you keep track of these strong and weak areas. (Students should keep these checklists in their folders for ready reference.) Proofread for anything the editors may have missed.

If students *are* ready for a conference, and if class time has run out, designate a place where writing is to be left, such as a writing box or folder.

You may decide to include an extra step in the system here—revision. This would be done only if major changes or additions were necessary in the rough draft.

Step 4: The Final Copy

Now the student makes a final copy, incorporating any suggestions made by the two peers and you. After you check and initial the final copy, it may be displayed in the class as a writing model for other students.

Encourage the workshop atmosphere! Use every available space for the materials and for displaying the writing activities. Spread them around the room so traffic flows rather than bunches in one area. If display space is limited, collect the writing in looseleaf binders and list all the titles of the writings on separate Contents pages.

To help keep track of the activities students have worked on, reproduce the Progress Sheet on page 12. As you return each final copy, you or the student can write the title on the tracking sheet. Students can keep these running inventories in their folders until the end of the term.

As students progress, they may want to try creating their *own* activities. Reproduce the form on page 11 and let your workshop thrive!

Remember, clear and effective writing begins with frequent practice. The *Ready-to-Use Writing Workshop Activities Kits* will turn your classroom into a productive workshop of aspiring readers, editors, advisors, decision makers—and writers!

WRITING WORKSHOP SYSTEM: STUDENT DIRECTIONS

Step 1: Do your *rough draft.*

Step 2: Get *two editors.*

Step 3: Ask for a *teacher conference* or leave your writing in the *writing box.*

Step 4: *Recopy* your writing, have it *checked,* and *display* it.

WRITING WORKSHOP EDITOR'S KEY

Here is a list of some common editing symbols. Use this proofreader's key whenever you are asked to be an editor. It will help you edit the writing sample.

SOME MARKINGS	HOW INDICATED IN COPY	THEIR MEANINGS
≡	come here. (c underlined with ≡)	Capitalize this letter.
/	Come Here. (H slashed)	Use a small letter instead of a capital.
∧	Is brekfast ready? (caret with "a" inserted)	This is a caret. Use it when you want to add a letter, word, or punctuation.
⊙	This is the end⊙	Add a period.
∧̓	After they left we slept.	Add a comma.
∧̇;	Don't go there it's late.	Add a semicolon.
∧:	such as peas, carrots, and corn.	Add a colon.
/	If the wrong punctuation is there/cross it out and write the correct one.	Change to the correct punctuation.
¶	end. Start a new line. (¶ inserted)	Make a new paragraph.
ʾʾ ʾʾ	ʾʾWalk with me, ʾʾ he said.	You need quotation marks.
⌢	basket ball (joined)	Join these two words or letters together.
—	Harry had two ~~big~~ huge sundaes.	Eliminate this word or letter.
—	John and Jane ~~was~~ were happy.	Eliminate this word or letter and use the one written above it.
∼	switch t⌒eh⌒/around⌐words⌐	Switch (transpose) the words or letters to the correct place.
|	I like ice cream a|lot.	Separate these words.

7

PRACTICE ACTIVITY FOR WRITING WORKSHOP

DIRECTIONS: This is a writing sample that will help you practice being an editor, the second step of the Writing Workshop. Write down one specific thing you like about this piece of writing. Ask one question that will help the writer clarify or expand something in the paragraph. Use your copy of the Writer's Workshop Editor's Key to help you proofread this writing. Then sign your name in the spot for "Editor 1" or "Editor 2."

(Writer's name) _____ Writing Workshop Rough Draft

(Editor #1) _____
I like _____

Question: _____

(Editor #2) _____
I like _____

Question: _____

Meet sally Brown

There is a girl named Sally Brown she move here with her parents. Some of the kids at school tease her because of the way she looks and her accent. When Sally told her parent's about her problem at school they said Oh, Sally, that happens to every new kid. Think about it. If you changed Sally's name to the name of some new kid in this school than you might stop and think before you tease him or her.

PRACTICE ACTIVITY FOR WRITING WORKSHOP—ANSWER KEY

DIRECTIONS: This is a writing sample that will help you practice being an editor, the second step of the Writing Workshop. Write down one specific thing you like about this piece of writing. Ask one question that will help the writer clarify or expand something in the paragraph. Use your copy of the Writer's Workshop Editor's Key to help you proofread this writing. Then sign your name in the spot for "Editor #1" or "Editor #2."

Dana Peters   Writing Workshop
(Writer's name)

Jane Ortiz   Rough Draft
(Editor #1)

I like the way you organized your sentences.

Question: How did Sally Brown look?

Tommy Jones
(Editor #2)

I like how you stayed on the topic.

Question: What kind of accent did Sally have?

Meet $\overset{S}{\cancel{s}}$ally Brown

→ There is a girl named Sally Brown. $\overset{S}{\cancel{s}}$he move$\overset{d}{\wedge}$ here$_\wedge$ with her parents. Some of the kids at
(When? From where?)
school tease her because of the way she looks$_\wedge$ (Her clothes? Her hair?)
and her$_\wedge$ accent. When Sally told her parent's
(What kind?)
about her problem at school they said$\overset{"}{,}$"Oh, Sally, that happens to every new kid$\overset{"}{.}$¶ Think about it. If you changed Sally's name to the name of some new kid in this school, th$\overset{e}{\cancel{a}}$n you might stop and think before you tease him or her.

WRITING WORKSHOP SURVEY

TO THE STUDENT: How do you feel about reading and editing another person's writing? It's important to remember the writer's feelings. Always look for at least one *good* point and write it down on the paper. Be specific with your comments. Was the writer clear? Were the adjectives descriptive? Will your comments help improve the writing piece?

    This survey is meant to help you think about choosing and being an editor. Do not sign your name. A class discussion will be held at a later time to discuss results of the survey.

1. I try to pick editors who _____

_____

_____

2. Whenever I am asked to be an editor, I feel _____

_____

_____

3. I would like to be an editor if _____

_____

_____

4. I might not want to be an editor if _____

_____

_____

5. When reading someone else's writing, I try to look for _____

_____

_____

6. I think good writing is _____

_____

_____

Name _____

Date _____

WRITE YOUR OWN ACTIVITY

TO THE STUDENT: Did you know that *you* are one of the best sources for ideas for writing? It's true! Here's your chance to create an original Writing Workshop Activity. All you have to do is fill in the section below. Then get your idea approved by the teacher. Once it's approved, you can start writing your own classroom activity!

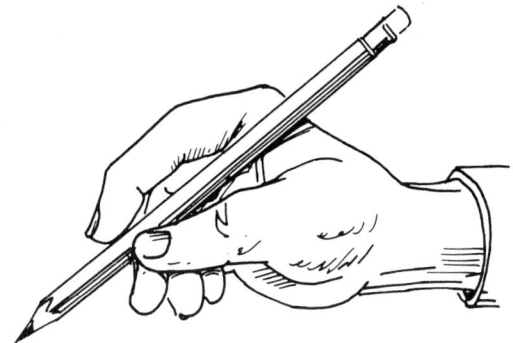

HINT: Need some ideas? Try looking through some old magazines, used workbooks, or textbooks.

I would like to design and make a writing activity. It would be about:
_____
_____
_____
_____

My title would be _____

My WARMING UP section (directions) would say _____
_____
_____

Some of my WRITING ACTIVITIES would be _____
_____
_____

I will need _____
_____

Approved by:

_____
(Teacher's Name)   (Date)

© 1985 by The Center for Applied Research in Education, Inc.

11

Name _____

Term   1   2   3   4

WRITING WORKSHOP PROGRESS SHEET

DIRECTIONS: This Progress Sheet will help student and teacher keep track of the activities the student has completed. The teacher should write the title of each activity on the tracking sheet below after the final copy has been returned to the student. The student can keep this sheet in his or her folder until the end of the term.

1. _____   16. _____
2. _____   17. _____
3. _____   18. _____
4. _____   19. _____
5. _____   20. _____
6. _____   21. _____
7. _____   22. _____
8. _____   23. _____
9. _____   24. _____
10. _____ 25. _____
11. _____ 26. _____
12. _____ 27. _____
13. _____ 28. _____
14. _____ 29. _____
15. _____ 30. _____

© 1985 by The Center for Applied Research in Education, Inc.

About Kit III

This *Kit* will help your students organize their thoughts into concise, informative paragraphs. Each of the 25 lessons offers entertaining and educational ideas for developing random words and phrases into cohesive and concise sentences and paragraphs. As a further aid to teaching, the lessons are divided into four main types of writing: descriptive, narrative, expository, and persuasive.

You can help your students familiarize themselves with the writing workshop system by reproducing and distributing the Writing Workshop Student Directions (page 6), the Editor's Key (page 7), and the sample editing practice activity (pages 8 and 9). Once they have mastered the four simple steps, your students will be ready to begin.

Lessons 1–17 deal with descriptive writing, with special emphasis on detail and sensory awareness. Lessons 8–13 feature narration as a writing tool, with dialogue, plot, and story viewpoint examined. Lessons 14–19 encourage students to explain their thoughts with details, facts, and original ideas. This expository writing section also touches upon problem-solving and analytical skills with activities such as "How Does It Work?" and "What Would You Do If…" Lessons 20–25 challenge the selling powers of your students by improving their persuasive writing skills. Writing radio commercials, campaign speeches, and advertisements for "Preposterous Products" are just a few of the activities offered.

A detailed Checklist for Paragraph Evaluation and Writing Conference is included in the back of this book for handy student and teacher use. Also included is a special skills index to help teachers quickly find the most effective writing lessons for their students.

You will find these lessons a valuable addition to your classroom writing workshop. Your students will also enjoy the variety of practical and challenging selections that prove once again—learning to write effectively can be fun!

Kit III
Paragraph Writing Skills
(Descriptive, Narrative, Expository, and Persuasive Writing)

About the *Ready-to-Use Writing Workshop Activities Kits*	1
How to Turn Your Classroom into a Writing Workshop	3
About Kit III	13

Lesson	Title	Skill	Page
DESCRIPTIVE WRITING			
III–1	Describe It	differentiating between similar objects	16
III–2	Setting the Scene	creating a realistic setting through sensory awareness	17
III–3	Mystery Description	describing familiar objects	18
III–4	Fingerprint File	comparing descriptions	19
III–5	Shoebox Personality	using paragraph form to describe personalities	20
III–6	Time Will Tell	using list and paragraph forms for animate and inanimate descriptions	21
III–7	Find the False Fact	more descriptions using list and paragraph forms	22
NARRATIVE WRITING			
III–8	Waking Hour	using phrases and dialogue in narrative story	23
III–9	Two Points of View	telling a story from different viewpoints; writing dialogue	24
III–10	If Things Could Talk	writing dialogue in paragraph style	25
III–11	Noun Story Starters	recognizing and using nouns as story ideas	26
III–12	Vampire!	encouraging fictitious writing with dialogue	27
III–13	Night Out	more practice with imaginative storytelling	28

Lesson	Title	Skill	Page
EXPOSITORY WRITING			
III–14	Tool Talk	explaining functions of inanimate objects	29
III–15	How Does It Work?	using details to explain common objects	30
III–16	What Would You Do If	solving problems and step-by-step explanation	31
III–17	Super Supper	creating and explaining a menu in sequential order	32
III–18	Favorite TV Series	describing plot through use of phrases and paragraphs	33
III–19	Careers	explaining the pros and cons of a profession	34
PERSUASIVE WRITING			
III–20	Come to My School	creating a newspaper article	35
III–21	Commercial Interruption	promoting a product by writing a radio commercial	36
III–22	Vote for Me!	writing a campaign speech	37
III–23	Preposterous Product	creating an advertisement	38
III–24	Sticky Situations	convincing another to think like you	39
III–25	The Wish Granter	selling yourself as a worthy recipient of a wish	40

Checklist for Paragraph Evaluation and Writing Conferences   41

Paragraph Writing Skills Index   44

III–1   Descriptive Writing   Name _____
                                    Date _____

DESCRIBE IT

Picture 1

Picture 2

WARMING UP: These two pictures seem alike, but if you look closely, you will notice some differences. Choose one picture and list those things about it that make it different from the other one.

1. I choose picture number _____.

2. The things that make it different from the other picture include:

_____
_____
_____
_____
_____

WRITING ACTIVITIES:

(A) Using your list from above, write a paragraph describing the picture you chose. Use the back of this paper.

(B) Pick two partners. Have each one guess from reading your paragraph which picture you are describing. Have them write their guesses next to their names below.

Reader 1: _____

I think the paragraph describes picture number _____.

Reader 2: _____

I think the paragraph describes picture number _____.

III–2   Descriptive Writing   Name _____

                                   Date _____

SETTING THE SCENE

WARMING UP: Whenever you write a story, your readers need to know when and where each part of the story takes place. When you describe these things, you are setting the scene. You can create a realistic setting for your readers if you describe sounds, sights, textures, shapes, and smells found in your settings.

WRITING ACTIVITIES:

(A) List eight things you could describe to set the scene in each of the following places.

JUNGLE: _____ _____ _____ _____
                  _____ _____ _____ _____

YOUR ROOM: _____ _____ _____ _____
                  _____ _____ _____ _____

SPACESHIP: _____ _____ _____ _____
                  _____ _____ _____ _____

SPORTS EVENT: _____ _____ _____ _____
                  _____ _____ _____ _____

SUPERMARKET: _____ _____ _____ _____
                  _____ _____ _____ _____

(B) Choose three of the settings from (A) above. Write a paragraph for each that describes only the setting. Use what you have written in the lists to help you write your paragraphs. Use separate paper.

III–3   **Descriptive Writing**   Name _____

Date _____

MYSTERY DESCRIPTION

WARMING UP: Descriptive detail will help your readers "see" the object you have written about.

WRITING ACTIVITIES:

(A) Look around the room in which you are sitting. Name ten things you can see.

1. _____
2. _____
3. _____
4. _____
5. _____
6. _____
7. _____
8. _____
9. _____
10. _____

(B) Choose one thing from the list in (A) and fill in the blanks below.

1. I have chosen _____.

2. Its color(s) is (are) _____.

3. Its shape is _____.

4. Its texture is _____.

5. Its form is _____.

6. Its weight is approximately _____.

7. Its function is _____.

(C) Using only the information in (B), 2–7, write a paragraph on separate paper describing the object you have chosen. Do not name the object.

(D) Pick two partners. Have each one guess what object you have described after reading your paragraphs. Have them write their guesses next to their names below.

Reader #1 _____   I think the paragraph describes _____
_____.

Reader #2 _____   I think the paragraph describes _____
_____.

III–4   Descriptive Writing   Name _____

                                    Date _____

FINGERPRINT FILE

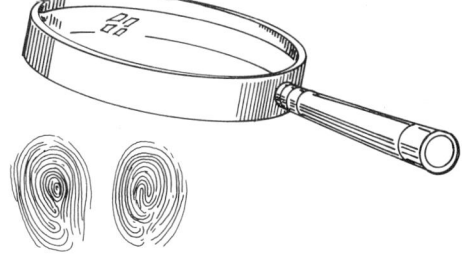

(To do this activity, you will need an inkpad, magnifying glass, and paper towels for cleaning ink off fingers.)

WARMING UP: There are no two fingerprints alike in the world! Look at the two fingerprints above and answer the following questions.

1. What are three differences you can see between the two fingerprints?

_____

_____

_____

2. Briefly describe the differences between the two fingerprints. Compare the lines, curves, and other characteristics to something you know, such as letters, numbers, waves, or a person's face.

Fingerprint 1   **Fingerprint 2**

_____   _____

_____   _____

_____   _____

WRITING ACTIVITIES:

(A) Pick a partner. Each of you should make a print of one of your own fingers or thumbs. Use a magnifying glass to examine your print carefully. Write a paragraph describing what you see. Be sure to specify which finger you have chosen.

(B) Now write a paragraph describing your partner's print. How does each differ? In what ways are they alike? Use as many descriptive words as you can.

III-5   Descriptive Writing   Name _____

Date _____

SHOEBOX PERSONALITY

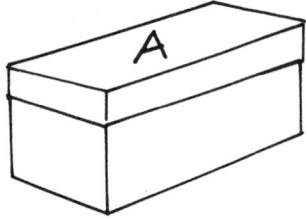 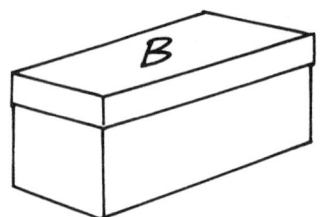 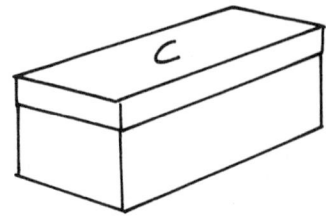

Person A

want ad from newspaper
pipe
electric razor
typewriter ribbon
tennis ball
credit cards
wallet
shopping list
sales slip for swing set

Person B

eyeglasses
knitting needles
bus token
magazine
plane ticket
Social Security check
grocery coupons
postage stamps
medicine

Person C

softball
notebook
cassette
pencil
chewing gum
ball pen
guitar pick
soda can
comb

WARMING UP: The three shoeboxes pictured above contain separate groups of articles that belong to _____, _____, and _____. My goodness, the identities of these people seem to have been misplaced! How will you "know" anything about them? See what you can figure out from the contents of each box.

WRITING ACTIVITY: Write a paragraph about each shoebox personality. Describe each one according to what you can guess about him or her from what is found in his or her shoebox. You should be able to guess such things as age, gender, interests, occupation. Use separate paper.

III–6   Descriptive Writing   Name _____

Date _____

TIME WILL TELL

WARMING UP: You are the clock here in the classroom. You have come to life and are able to see some interesting goings-on. You want to talk about it, but you have no mouth. Well, even though you have no mouth, you do have hands with which to write.

WRITING ACTIVITIES:

(A) List ten things and/or persons you notice as you look down into this room.

1. _____
2. _____
3. _____
4. _____
5. _____
6. _____
7. _____
8. _____
9. _____
10. _____

(B) Use the list you have just written to help you write your description of this room. Use paragraph form.

III–7 Descriptive Writing   Name _____

                                Date _____

FIND THE FALSE FACT

WARMING UP: Read this paragraph about bats.

Bats are fascinating creatures. They are nocturnal animals, which means they are active at night. Most species live in caves, hanging from the walls by clinging to rough spots with their teeth. When they fly, they make a high-pitched squeaking sound. This sound bounces off objects, thereby warning them to fly away from the objects.

WRITING ACTIVITIES:

(A) What is the "false fact" in this paragraph? _____

_____. (The answer is given at the bottom of the page.)

(B) Name an animal about which you know at least four facts. _____

(C) List four facts that describe this animal.

1. _____   3. _____
2. _____   4. _____

(D) Write down one "false fact" you can make up about this animal.

_____

(E) On the back of this paper, write a paragraph describing the animal you have chosen. Include the four facts you wrote above as well as the "false fact" you made up. When you have completed the paragraph, take it to a partner and have him or her read the paragraph carefully. Your partner should then write down his or her name below and guess which one of the facts is "false."
For example:

PARTNER'S NAME _____

I think the false fact is _____

_____

FALSE FACT: Bats hang by their feet, not by their teeth.

22

© 1985 by The Center for Applied Research in Education, Inc.

III–8 Narrative Writing   Name _____

Date _____

WAKING HOUR

 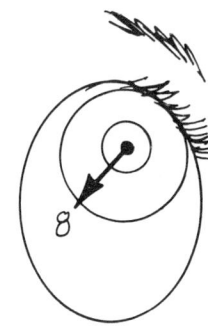

WARMING UP: It is this morning. You are fast asleep. You wake up.

1. What makes you wake up? _____
   _____

2. What time is it when you awaken? _____

3. Try to recall these details:

   a. List, in phrase form, what happened during your WAKING HOUR.

   _____   _____
   _____   _____
   _____   _____
   _____   _____

   b. List all the people whose voices you heard during your WAKING HOUR.

   _____   _____
   _____   _____
   _____   _____

WRITING ACTIVITY: On separate paper, write the story of your WAKING HOUR. Include dialogue that you can remember. Use what you have written in the WARMING UP section to help you develop your narration.

III-9   Narrative Writing   Name _____

Date _____

TWO POINTS OF VIEW

WARMING UP: A narration about the same event can be very different depending on who is telling the story.

All I did was knock over a lamp. Sarah and I were just fooling around a little when it happened. It was just an accident, and I'm sorry it broke. When my mother walked into the room, I knew I would get hollered at. She yelled, "Now look what you have done! Because of your carelessness, you're grounded for one week."

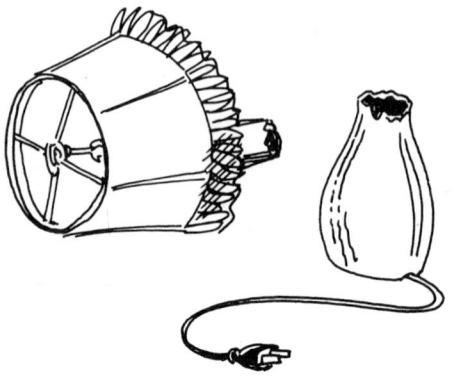

If I've told her once, I've told her a thousand times: no rough behavior in the living room! When I walked into the house, I heard the yelling, bumping, and running. Then, crash! I tried to keep my temper and managed to say in a calm but firm voice, "Now look what you have done. Because of your carelessness, you're grounded for one week."

Who is the speaker in the first paragraph? _____

Who is the speaker in the second paragraph? _____

How are the two narrations alike? _____

How are they different? _____

WRITING ACTIVITY: Choose an event from the list below. Tell the same story two times: once from each person's point of view. Include dialogue in your paragraphs. Write your narration on separate paper.

(A) a new baby being brought into the house
    characters: baby and an older brother or sister
(B) student bringing home his or her report card
    characters: student and student's parent
(C) buying some new clothes with your mother or father
    characters: you and your parent
(D) playing a team sport
    characters: winning team member and losing team member

© 1985 by The Center for Applied Research in Education, Inc.

III–10   Narrative Writing   Name _____

Date _____

IF THINGS COULD TALK

WARMING UP: Name one thing that fits into each category.

1. a plant _____
2. a wild animal _____
3. a domesticated animal _____
4. a tool _____
5. a machine _____
6. a toy _____
7. an article of clothing _____
8. a piece of sporting equipment _____
9. an appliance _____
10. a mineral _____

WRITING ACTIVITY: The things you have named above are unable to speak. Choose one and write what it might say to you if it could. Use paragraph form. (You can write on the back of this paper if you need more space.)

_____
_____
_____
_____
_____
_____

III–11   **Narrative Writing**   Name _____

Date _____

NOUN STORY STARTERS

WARMING UP: Nouns name persons, places, and things. Place each noun below in the correct category.

knife	banker	highway
scientist	camera	spaceship
desert	city	pin
trash can	winner	street
cab driver	television set	singer
race track	Detroit	kids
plate	rose	senior citizen
salesperson	sculptor	dirt bike
Germany	backyard	hot rod
Mars	police officer	park

PERSONS　　　　　　　　　**PLACES**　　　　　　　　　**THINGS**

_____　　_____　　_____
_____　　_____　　_____
_____　　_____　　_____
_____　　_____　　_____
_____　　_____　　_____
_____　　_____　　_____
_____　　_____　　_____
_____　　_____　　_____
_____　　_____　　_____
_____　　_____　　_____

WRITING ACTIVITIES:

(A) Choose one noun from each category. Write your choices below.

_____   _____   _____

Think about how they could all fit into the action or plot of a story.

(B) Write your story and underline your three word choices every time you use them. Use separate paper.

© 1985 by The Center for Applied Research in Education, Inc.

III–12   Narrative Writing

VAMPIRE!

WARMING UP:

Name the most famous vampire you have heard or read about.

Describe two things this vampire is able to do because he is a vampire.

1. _____
2. _____

Describe two things he is unable to do because he is a vampire.

1. _____
2. _____

Tell one way to keep a vampire away or to kill him.

_____

WRITING ACTIVITIES:

Choose one of the writing activities from below. Tell your story in paragraph form. Include dialogue between your characters. Use separate paper.

(A) Create your own vampire. Tell the story of one night in his or her life.
(B) Tell the story of how the first vampire came to be.
(C) You are attending a party. You have just met someone and you are certain he or she is a vampire. What happens?

III–13   **Narrative Writing**   Name _____

Date _____

NIGHT OUT

☆ ☆ ☆ ☆ ☆ ☆ ☆ ☆ ☆ ☆

WARMING UP: Write down the names of five famous people you would like most to meet.

an athlete _____   a political leader _____

a movie star _____   a television star _____

a musical star _____   your choice _____

You have the choice of spending an evening with **one** of the famous people you have named. Answer the questions below to help you get started.

1. How would you get to go on this "night out" in the first place?

   _____

   _____

2. Where would you decide to spend the evening? _____

   _____

3. What would you talk about? _____

   _____

   _____

   _____

4. What would you wear? _____

   _____

WRITING ACTIVITY: Your "night out" has come and gone. It's the next day. Use your answers from the exercise above to help you begin your paragraph/s telling what happened during your "night out." Use separate paper.

© 1985 by The Center for Applied Research in Education, Inc.

III–14 Expository Writing   Name _____

Date _____

TOOL TALK

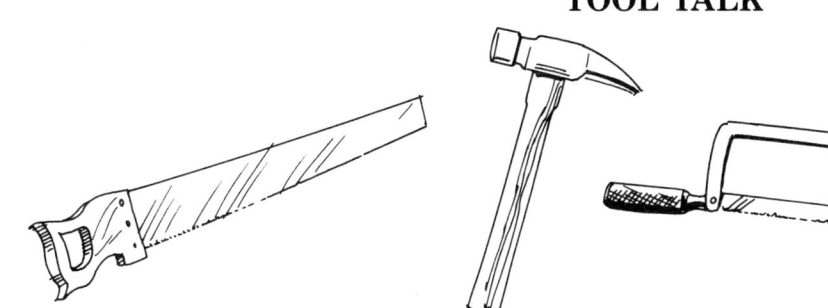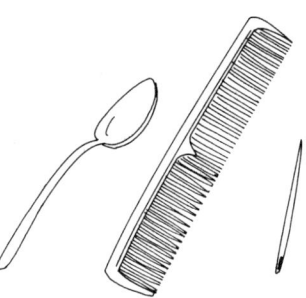

WARMING UP: A tool is used to do work but, unlike a machine, has no moving parts. Name five tools you have used at home or at school.

1. _____   4. _____

2. _____   5. _____

3. _____

WRITING ACTIVITY: Explain the purposes for which each tool you named above is designed. Use paragraph form as you explain the functions of the tools you have named.

_____
_____
_____
_____
_____
_____
_____
_____
_____
_____
_____
_____
_____
_____

III-15   Expository Writing   Name _____

Date _____

HOW DOES IT WORK?

WARMING UP: Look at the drawings above. About which one do you know the most?

I know the most about the _____.

List as many facts as you can about the item you have named, telling how you think it works.

_____
_____
_____
_____
_____
_____
_____

WRITING ACTIVITY: Use the information you have listed above to begin your paragraph explaining how the object you have chosen works. Use separate paper.

III–16 Expository Writing

WHAT WOULD YOU DO IF...

WARMING UP: What would you do to solve each of the problems below?

1. What would you do if you discovered an alligator in your bathtub?

2. What would you do if you found out that your best friend was an alien from another planet?

3. What would you do if you were lost in a strange city?

4. What would you do if you accidentally overheard a plot to rob a bank?

5. What would you do if the ten dollars you put in your pocket this morning was missing?

6. What would you do if you could get rid of any four shows on television?

WRITING ACTIVITY: Using paragraph form, write down on separate paper a complete, step-by-step solution to **one** of the problems you have written about in the WARMING UP section.

III–17   Expository Writing   Name _____

Date _____

SUPER SUPPER

WARMING UP: You have just been told that you can order a SUPER SUPPER made up of all your favorite foods!

1. Where would your SUPER SUPPER take place? _____

2. Who would serve your SUPER SUPPER? _____

3. What foods would be included in your SUPER SUPPER?

   a. appetizers: _____

   ingredients: _____

   b. soup: _____

   ingredients: _____

   c. main course: _____

   ingredients: _____

   d. beverages: _____

   ingredients: _____

   e. desserts: _____

   ingredients: _____

WRITING ACTIVITY: On separate paper, write about your SUPER SUPPER from start to finish in paragraph form. Use all of the information you have written in the WARMING UP section.

III–18 **Expository Writing**

FAVORITE TV SERIES

WARMING UP: Do you look forward to one particular television show each week? Think about one recent episode of your favorite television series.

1. The show I have chosen is _____.

2. The main characters in this episode were _____
_____.

3. List in order the plot or action of one particular episode you have rememberd. Use phrases, rather than sentences.

_____
_____
_____
_____
_____
_____
_____
_____
_____
_____

WRITING ACTIVITY: Using paragraph form, write down on separate paper a full explanation of the plot you have listed above.

III–19   **Expository Writing**   Name _____

Date _____

CAREERS

WARMING UP: If a person intends to work at the same kind of job for a long time, then we say that the person has picked a career. This is an important decision to make because it usually means taking the time to be trained to do that job. Read this list of jobs some people do:

medical technician	lumberjack	professional sportsperson
doctor	computer programmer	banker
nurse	salesperson	musician
teacher	farmer	_____ (your choice)

Do you know more about one of the careers listed above than the others? Chances are, then, that you either know someone who works at that job or you have an interest in that career yourself.

1. Of all the careers mentioned above, I know the most about _____
_____.

2. Five advantages in picking this career are: _____
_____
_____.

3. Some problems or hazards on this job are: _____
_____.

4. The training needed for this career is _____
_____.

5. A person choosing this career should have these qualities: _____
_____
_____.

WRITING ACTIVITY: Use the information you have written above to help you begin explaining, in paragraph form, what it means to have picked that career. Use separate paper.

III–20   Persuasive Writing   Name _____

Date _____

COME TO MY SCHOOL

WARMING UP: Suppose that students could choose to attend any school they wished. To help students make their decision, each school has been asked to submit an article to the local newspaper that explains all the advantages of attending that school.

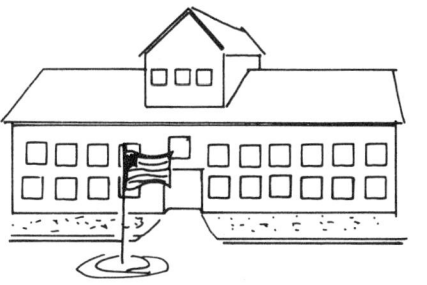

You have been chosen to write an article telling how great your school is. Finish the statements below to help you get started.

1. The full name of my school is _____.

2. My school has the best _____
   _____.

3. Some things that my school has that others don't have are _____
   _____.

4. Some problems my school has solved are _____
   _____.

5. Some things about my school that we are making better include _____
   _____
   _____.

WRITING ACTIVITY: Use your answers from the exercise above to write your own article. It should be in paragraph form. Use separate paper.

III-21   Persuasive Writing   Name _____

Date _____

COMMERCIAL INTERRUPTION

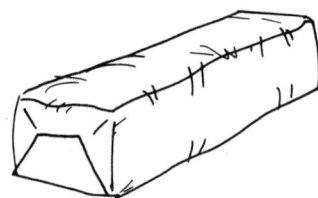 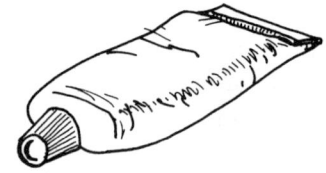  

WARMING UP: Make up your own brand names for an item in each product category:

1. _____   3. _____   5. _____
   (snack)   (toothpaste)   (your choice)

2. _____   4. _____
   (soap)   (jeans)

You have been hired to write a radio commercial for one product you have named above. List below what makes your brand better than all the others so that anyone listening to your commercial will buy your brand from now on.

_____ is better because:
(brand name of your product)

1. _____
2. _____
3. _____
4. _____
5. _____

WRITING ACTIVITY: Write your radio commercial below in paragraph form using the information from the WARMING UP section.

_____
_____
_____
_____
_____
_____

III-22   Persuasive Writing   Name _____

Date _____

VOTE FOR ME!

WARMING UP: You are a candidate in a school election. List five reasons why you would be the **best** candidate. If elected, what would you do to improve the club, organization, or team you wish to represent? What would you do for your fellow students?

I am the best candidate for _____
(office)

_____ because:
(name of club, organization, or team)

1. _____
2. _____
3. _____
4. _____
5. _____

WRITING ACTIVITY: Write your campaign speech in paragraph form using the information listed above.

_____
_____
_____
_____
_____
_____
_____
_____

III–23   Persuasive Writing   Name _____
                                     Date _____

PREPOSTEROUS PRODUCT

WARMING UP: Read this list of preposterous products:
a. a pad of paper already filled with writing
b. a robot that cannot move
c. a record album with no sound on it
d. a box of sealed, empty envelopes
e. a candy bar with no flavor

f. _____
   (your choice)

What possible uses could these foolish products have? Who could be persuaded to buy them? Pick *one* product from the list above and think about what you would say to convince someone to buy it. Then write:

I could sell _____ to _____
             (which preposterous product)   (which kind of person)

The reasons I would give to convince the person to buy this product would be:

1. _____
2. _____
3. _____
4. _____
5. _____

WRITING ACTIVITY: Use the ideas you have written above to write an advertisement for your preposterous product. Write your ad in paragraph form and illustrate it on another sheet of paper.

STICKY SITUATIONS

WARMING UP: Suppose you had to talk someone into doing (or not doing) something. Suppose someone thinks something is true, but you *know* it isn't. For example:

1. Someone has told your best friend that you said something awful about him or her.
2. While babysitting, one of your friends calls you and wants you to have a party where you are babysitting.
3. Some of your friends want you to go to a place with them, but you have been forbidden to go there by your parents.
4. A stranger walks up to you and insists that he knows you.
5. Your friend tells you that he or she is planning to run away from home.
6. _____
   (your choice)

_____

Pick **one** of the sticky situations from above and circle it.

The arguments I could give to convince the person/s to think my way are:

1. _____
2. _____
3. _____
4. _____

WRITING ACTIVITY: On separate paper, write a paragraph in which you try to persuade the other person to do what you want. Use the arguments you have listed in the WARMING UP section.

III–25   Persuasive Writing   Name _____

Date _____

THE WISH GRANTER

WARMING UP: One morning you awaken to the sound of a voice that says to you: "I am the Wish Granter and you are to be granted **one** wish. You will receive your wish if you can convince me that you really deserve it. You must think of five reasons why your wish should be granted. I will return in twenty-four hours." Then the voice stops.

1. How would you decide what your one wish will be? _____
   _____

2. What would your wish be? _____
   _____

3. What five reasons would you give the Wish Granter as proof that you deserve to have this wish granted?

   a. _____
   b. _____
   c. _____
   d. _____
   e. _____

WRITING ACTIVITY: It is twenty-four hours later. Use paragraph form to describe what is happening between you and the Wish Granter. Use the ideas you have written in the WARMING UP section.

© 1985 by The Center for Applied Research in Education, Inc.

How to Use the Checklist for Paragraph Evaluation and Writing Conferences

There are two main reasons for using this checklist: first, as a guide, and second, as a basis for individual writing conferences with the students.

As a "teacher's guide," it helps you in evaluating the strengths and weaknesses of your students' paragraph writing.

Each student should also have a copy of this reproducible checklist for ready reference. As you read the student's writing, you can place the pertinent numbers of the items from the checklist at the top or in the margins of the paper. Then you leave the paper with the student so that the student can make any changes in the specified areas himself or herself. You may then return at a later time to discuss the alterations and complete the writing conference. This self-checking improves students' editorial skills and allows for more productive writing conferences.

KIT III: CHECKLIST FOR PARAGRAPH EVALUATION AND WRITING CONFERENCE

1. Center your title on the line and capitalize the important words.
2. Indent the first word in each paragraph.
3. You need a topic sentence that generally tells the reader what the rest of the paragraph will be about. Your remaining sentences should give specific details that support your topic sentence.
4. Skip a line between your title and the opening paragraph.
5. A title does not need a period at the end of it.
6. Start a new paragraph when you shift to a new idea.
7. When writing dialogue, start a new paragraph when you change speakers.
8. Vary your sentence length by mixing some shorter, more dramatic sentences with some longer ones.
9. You have some run-on sentences. Find and rework them.
10. Many of your sentences begin the same way. Try to vary them.
11. Combine the information in some of your shorter sentences into longer compound ones. Use conjunctions such as: and, but, however, consequently, or, either, nor, neither, if, because, whenever, after, although.
12. You have some sentence fragments that are not part of a dialogue or interior monologue. Find and rework them.
13. Punctuate all of the necessary words and sentences.
14. Capitalize and underline all of the necessary words.
15. You need to punctuate your dialogue and capitalize the first word in each quotation.
16. You have used some words incorrectly. Look up any of the words that you are not sure of or use more familiar ones.
17. Your opening should make the reader want to read the rest of the paragraph. You can rework it by asking a question, using an appropriate quotation or dialogue, or hinting about something unusual that is about to happen.
18. Who is telling this story? Is it written in first person (I), second person (you), or third person (it, he, she, they)? It should be the same throughout your composition.
19. You can make your setting more real by describing sound, sights, smells, or textures where your action takes place.
20. Make your dialogue sound more natural. Do your characters always speak in the same way, or do their voices change as the action takes place? Is there a dialect you can reproduce to make them seem more alive?
21. Your actions, ideas, or arguments need to be arranged in a more sequential, logical order.

22. Add or substitute some adjectives in your writing to help the reader draw a better mental picture of your characters and setting.

23. Add or substitute some adverbs or adverbial phrases to help your readers draw a better mental picture of how the action is taking place in your story.

24. You can leave out some part/s of this and still say what you want to say.

25. Support some of your general statements with more details and/or proofs.

26. You can vary the verb or add an adverb to identify the way in which a character speaks. For example, John *said,* "Put that book down." becomes John screamed, "Put that book down!" or John said excitedly, "Put that book down!"

27. Revise this ending. You can summarize what you have said, ask a series of questions, or surprise your readers.

28. Who is the "he", "she", or "it" you are talking about? Name your character or main idea, and then you can use the pronoun.

29. You can describe your character/s more completely. Does a character move in an odd or certain way, have an unusual voice, or have a notable physical characteristic?

30. Your subject and verb do not always agree. Please find where and revise them.

Paragraph Writing Skills Index

ADVERTISEMENTS

Commercial Interruption	36
Preposterous Product	38

ANTHROPOMORPHISM (Giving inanimate objects human characteristics)

If Things Could Talk	25
Time Will Tell	21
Tool Talk	29

COMPARISONS

Describe It	16
Fingerprint File	19

DESCRIPTIVE WRITING

Describe It	16
Find the "False" Fact	22
Fingerprint File	19
Mystery Description	18
Setting the Scene	17
Shoebox Personality	20
Time Will Tell	21

DIALOGUE

If Things Could Talk	25
Two Points of View	24
Vampire!	27
Waking Hour	23

EXPOSITORY WRITING

Careers	34
Favorite TV Series	33
How Does it Work?	30
Tool Talk	29
What Would You Do If	31
Super Supper	32

KIT III: PARAGRAPH WRITING SKILLS

FAMOUS PEOPLE OR STORY CHARACTERS, DESCRIBING

Favorite TV Series 33
Night Out 28
Vampire! 27

FICTION

Night Out 28
Vampire! 27

NARRATIVE WRITING

If Things Could Talk 25
Night Out 28
Noun Story Starters 26
Two Points of View 24
Vampire! 27
Waking Hour 23

PERSUASIVE WRITING

Come to My School 35
Commercial Interruption 36
Preposterous Product 38
Sticky Situations 39
Vote for Me! 37
The Wish Granter 40

PERSONALITY, DEFINING

Shoebox Personality 20

PLOT

Favorite TV Series 33
Noun Story Starters 26

PROBLEM SOLVING

What Would You Do If 31

PUBLIC RELATIONS

Come to My School 35